Vinnie and Me

By Rosalind Malam

Illustrated by Karen Oppatt

Vinnie and Me

The Bombshell

OK, so I'm one of the lucky ones. Life had chewed me thoroughly then spat me out again – and I had survived. More than that, I had landed on my feet. Yet sometimes . . . I wished things could be a little different.

You see, my parents take in foster kids until their home situations are more stable. Fair enough. I had needed a helping hand, too. But how would you like to share your room, your family and chunks of your entire life with a parcel of strangers? Exactly!

...I wished thing

Predict What might happen in this story?

...uld be a little different...

Question Generate   What questions could you ask about the narrator?

On this particular occasion, I was surfing the Net, collecting information about sea mammals for my school project. Summer had elbowed in ahead of schedule, and my mind was humming with plans. Then the phone rang.

Another guest was roller-coasting in my direction.

As usual the timing couldn't have been worse – school holidays had just started.

"Let me guess," I groaned when Mum came to explain. "An ankle-biter's on its way! Or is it a buddy around my age to brighten up my holiday?"

Ankle-biters are bad news, but probably the lesser of the two evils. When they're not teasing the dog or terrorising the cat, they specialise in full-throttle tantrums, cunningly timed to destroy my favourite TV programmes! Our last ankle-biter was an expert – I'm sure he broke the sound barrier!

Vinnie's mute...

Clarify   **full-throttle tantrums**

"Actually, Robbie, Vinnie is your age," Mum replied calmly.

"Brilliant!" I moaned. "I'll bet he won't meddle with my stuff or wreck my collections – and I suppose his tongue isn't on fast forward either!" (My last "buddy" had followed me like a footprint, chattering away as if tomorrow had been cancelled. Visits to the bathroom were my only escape.)

Then Mum really dropped the bombshell.

"Vinnie's mute, Robbie. He doesn't talk at all."

Literary Device

Then Mum really dropped the bombshell.

idiom or metaphor?

idiom = a common phrase that doesn't make sense when read literally (with its actual meaning)

metaphor = a phrase that compares one thing to another to create a mind picture

Vinnie

Vinnie arrived the following morning. His caregiver dumped a battered suitcase and speedily departed. I looked Vinnie over in disbelief. No way could this weed of a kid be the same age as me!

Vinnie glanced at us briefly, then down at his grubby sneakers. Tumbled curls flopped across anxious eyes, shielding him from the awkwardness of the moment. Head down and shoulders hunched, he looked hopelessly vulnerable in his shabby, ill-fitting clothes.

Dad put a hand on his shoulder.

"Hi, Vinnie," he said. "Welcome to our patch."

The remainder of the day was difficult, to say the least. Imagine trying to connect with someone who pulls down the shutters every time you try to get through!

My initial sympathy for Vinnie was gone before lunchtime. He shovelled food in, barely pausing to chew, then swallowed it down in gulps that were painful to watch. He reminded me of Havoc, our Labrador retriever, greedily guzzling his breakfast.

I looked

Literary Devices

metaphor   simile

alliteration   idiom

Are there any?

...Vinnie over in disbelief...

Somehow we waded through the afternoon, but by evening my attitude had softened again. Vinnie had relaxed a bit, and when Mum suggested that I show him my sea mammal project, he examined it with interest. We enjoyed the same TV programmes and Havoc – who always seems to know which characters are best avoided – had accepted Vinnie already.

When bedtime came, though, Vinnie looked as lost as an abandoned teddy bear. I encouraged Havoc to curl up beside his bed, hoping he'd be of some comfort.

Imagery

Somehow we waded through the afternoon, but by evening my attitude had softened again.

Use the words to create your own mind picture.

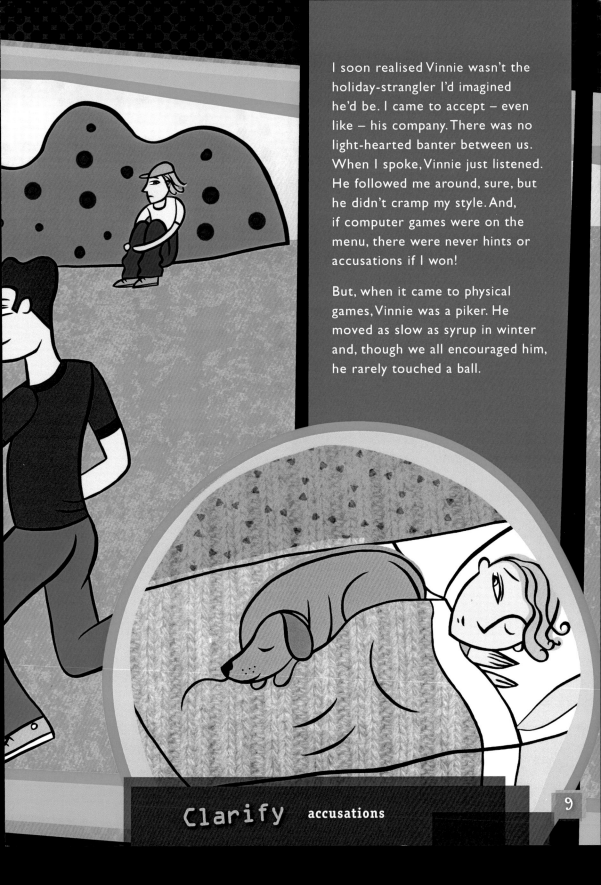

I soon realised Vinnie wasn't the holiday-strangler I'd imagined he'd be. I came to accept – even like – his company. There was no light-hearted banter between us. When I spoke, Vinnie just listened. He followed me around, sure, but he didn't cramp my style. And, if computer games were on the menu, there were never hints or accusations if I won!

But, when it came to physical games, Vinnie was a piker. He moved as slow as syrup in winter and, though we all encouraged him, he rarely touched a ball.

Clarify accusations

Wind Dancer

"Guess what, boys," said Mum, two weeks into Vinnie's visit. "Uncle Laurie's just invited us to sail on his boat tomorrow. We leave before sunrise."

"C-o-o-o-l!" I exclaimed, though a hint of a shadow had crossed Vinnie's face. Uncle Laurie's little yacht, *Wind Dancer*, is his pride and joy, and he just loves sharing it.

"Hey, Vinnie, we might get to spot some sea mammals – seals or maybe even dolphins," I suggested. I knew the dolphin bit was unlikely, but I wanted to pass on a little bit of my own enthusiasm.

We arrived at the jetty just as the sun rose and lazily stretched itself across the morning sky. I was nearly jumping with excitement as Uncle Laurie backed the trailer down the ramp, immersing *Wind Dancer*'s hull in the water. Beside me, Vinnie shivered with excitement, too – at least that's what I hoped it was – and Dad beckoned us over.

"Boys, hold the bow-line while I push her into the water. Here she goes . . . "

Whoosh!

Wind Dancer slid from the trailer and we hauled her towards the jetty. Dad was first to board the yacht and he started up the motor.

"Young man, you have the look of an able seaman," said Uncle Laurie, beaming as he helped Vinnie on board and then followed himself. Pleased with this unexpected praise, Vinnie walked steadily across the gently rocking deck and sat down on the cockpit squab. I staggered over to join him, then Mum and Havoc were the last to clamber aboard.

Inference   What does ...a hint of shadow had crossed Vinnie's face ... imply about Vinnie's mood?

Literary Devices

onomatopoeia =
a word that sounds like
the thing it describes

malapropism =
using the wrong word

Are there any?

"Avast ye, matie!"

We listened to the steady borm-borm-borm of the throbbing engine, powering us out from the jetty.

"Avast ye, matie!" I said, grinning and digging Vinnie in the ribs. Vinnie smiled shyly back and settled down to enjoy the unfamiliar motion as *Wind Dancer* cut through the waves.

"One day I'll be as effluent as you, Unc, and own my own yacht," I shouted over to Uncle Laurie at the tiller, wondering at the howls of laughter that followed.

"Don't you mean affluent...as in rich?" asked Uncle Laurie, chortling. "Effluent is...well, look it up in the dictionary when you get home!"

Inference

What can you infer about the character of Robbie from this dialogue?
"Avast ye, matie!"

Character Analysis

What sort of character do you think Uncle Laurie is?

Now that we were far enough from the jetty, it was time to set the sails. Dad pulled the halyard to hoist up the mainsail. It quickly caught the breeze, flapping wildly like a seabird against the wind.

Uncle Laurie turned off the engine, put down the keel and hoisted the foresail. For a while, we enjoyed the tranquillity of the ocean. The only sounds were the cries of the gulls and the gentle swoosh of the waves against *Wind Dancer*'s hull.

Nervous Wreck

Predict   What do you think will happen in this chapter?

"Like a turn at the tiller?" asked Uncle Laurie. He didn't need to ask twice!

For a while, we took turns, steering *Wind Dancer* towards Mariner's Cove on the outskirts of the harbour. Uncle Laurie adjusted the foresail, angling the boat to the wind. Now we were going faster, and on a lean ... which was scary at first.

"Don't worry, Vinnie, she won't tip over," I assured him. But Vinnie wasn't looking worried! He was already behaving like a seasoned sailor, rising like the waves to the challenges around him.

He seemed to be revelling in the experience.

Being on the water and looking at the land – everything was so different. It's a calming atmosphere, and we were basking in it ... the hushing sounds of the sea, glittering in the sunshine as if it were covered with sequins ... watching out for jumping fish and diving seabirds ... or just staring out at the smoky horizon.

14

Clarify   revelling

Literary Devices

metaphor   simile

idiom
onomatopoeia

alliteration

Are there any?

Character Analysis

How does the author show that Vinnie is now confident?

"Are you hungry, guys?" asked Mum. "Then go down to the galley and bring up the chillybin."

"Pour us some drinks, please, while you're at it," added Dad. "I'll ease off the mainsail to slow us, and straighten up the lean."

Between lurches, Vinnie and I inched down the cockpit hatchway to the galley below.

Soon we were back on deck, dangling our legs under the starboard railing, munching chicken sandwiches and Mum's famous chocolate cake. Our feet caught the occasional burst of spray.

"Hey, Vinnie! What lies at the bottom of the sea and shivers?" I demanded. In these beautiful surroundings, I half expected an answer, but Vinnie just looked at me inquiringly.

"A nervous wreck!" I answered myself, and Vinnie gave a little chuckle.

In all the time he'd been with us, this was a first!

16

Question

How do you think Vinnie feels about being on the boat? Why?

...a little chuckle...

Vinnie's surprise

character Prediction

What do you think Vinnie's surprise will be?

Wind Dancer resumed her rhythm as Uncle Laurie guided her into the bay. He dropped the anchor while Dad furled the sails.

Then I spotted it... a huge dorsal fin, appearing without warning just metres from our boat. Sharks! I thought about shrieking a warning, but I seemed to be paralysed with fear. Then, before I could get out a sound, an excited whisper reached my ear...

"Robbie, look! Dolphins!"

I looked – and there they were, a huge pod of them, swiftly circling that enchanted bay. Suddenly there were gasps and exclamations. Dad's camera was flashing, hands were waving, fingers pointing, voices raised.

I was so captivated by the dolphins, it was a while before I realised what had just happened.

Vinnie had broken his silence! And I'd been the first to hear him talk.

Clarify

furled
intricate

Robbie, look! Dolphins!

Working as a team, the dolphins were feeding – slapping their tails to drive fish into the shallow waters. Then, as they became aware of our presence, the pod swam over to cruise around *Wind Dancer*, tumbling like acrobats in the waves.

Their glistening bodies soared ... leaping, arching and diving together. Hurtling through the water, they raced and chased, making intricate patterns like weavers at a tapestry.

19

Alongside the railing, a dolphin surfaced, regarding me with a bright, curious eye. Suddenly it exhaled from its blow-hole…

Porfffff!

The noise was like an explosion – a massive beach ball deflating – and we were peppered with spray. I got such a shock that I grabbed hold of Vinnie, and we leaned back, laughing, against the railing. The dolphin's curved mouth smiled up at us, as if it were enjoying the joke, too!

I begged to be allowed to swim with the pod and, to my delight, the answer was yes! I turned to look for Vinnie, sad that he wouldn't be able to share this incredible experience. But I was in for another shock! Vinnie had already tossed aside his T-shirt and was looking at me expectantly, all set to leap from the stern!

…I was in for anothe

Literary Devices

metaphor
simile
idiom
onomatopoeia
alliteration

Are there any?

Dancing with the Dolphins

Vinnie moved like a fish in the waves, calmly and easily – better than I did! I was amazed that such an awkward figure on land could be so nimble and agile in the water.

One huge dolphin – probably a male – swam towards us while the other dolphins retreated. I guessed that, as head of the pod, he'd come to check us out. He moved forwards swiftly, circling and eyeballing us inquisitively before rejoining the pod.

Then suddenly they were all streaking towards us, tail-walking, leap-frogging, inviting us to play. Smooth and sleek, their streamlined bodies wove between us, making us laugh in surprise and delight!

We trod the water and ducked beneath the waves – spluttering, chuckling – enjoying every moment with our amazing company.

A little calf swam with the pod, gleefully tossing seaweed clusters and gliding around the two of us as joyfully as the rest.

Clarify   **nimble and agile**

Time galloped past. When Uncle Laurie shouted over that it was time to set sail again, the dolphins were as reluctant for us to go as we were to leave them! As we sailed out of the bay, many of them zigzagged in front of *Wind Dancer*'s bow, as if they were trying to stop us going! Others were bow-riding, while some cruised in the wake or glided in alongside the hull.

The baby dolphin frolicked beside us, flopping endearingly onto its back and revealing a smooth white underbelly. All around us, the ocean heaved with dolphins ... darting, diving, dissecting the water with their sharp dorsal fins.

Twice, fizz-boats passed within calling distance, gunning their engines and speeding around us, hoping to lure the dolphins away ... hoping to entice them to their vessels. But the dolphins had bonded with Vinnie and me and they stayed with us.

the ocean heaved with dolphins ...

Give Your opinion

Do you think the fizz-boats should be trying to lure the dolphins?

Why or why not?

Literary Devices

metaphor

simile

idiom

onomatopoeia   alliteration

personification

Are there any?

Character Analysis

How has the relationship between Vinnie and Robbie developed?

It had been an awesome adventure – the experience of a lifetime. Vinnie sat beside me, quietly content, as *Wind Dancer* re-entered the harbour.

I thought about those precious moments when I first realised he'd spoken. Vinnie's future was an unwritten page, and I was hoping I'd be part of it. But right now his heart was still out there at sea… **dancing with the dolphins.**

…his heart was still out

character comparison Diagram

Robbie

Vinnie

Confident

?

?

?

Shy

...there at sea...

Think about the Text

What connections can you make to the emotions, situations or characters in *Vinnie and Me*?

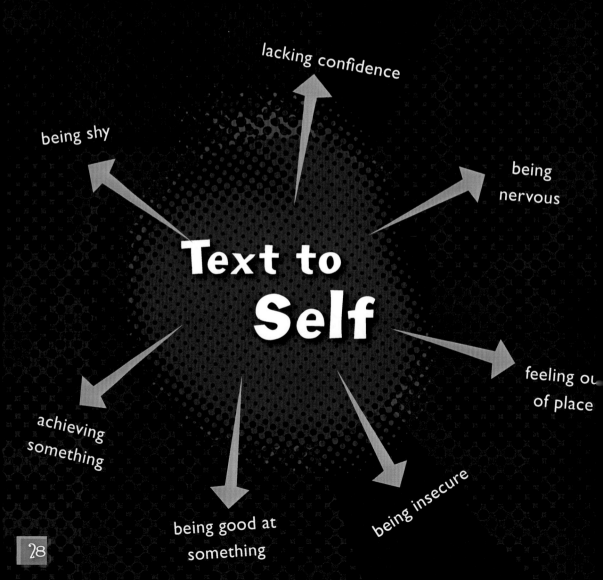

lacking confidence

being shy

being nervous

Text to Self

feeling ou[t] of place

achieving something

being insecure

being good at something

Text to Text

Talk about other stories you may have read that have similar features. Compare the stories.

Text to World

Talk about situations in the world that might connect to elements in the story.

Planning a Personal Recount

1 Think about an introduction.

WHO → Robbie and Vinnie

WHEN → When Vinnie came to stay

WHERE → At Robbie's house

WHAT → Vinnie is mute

2 Think about events in order of time.

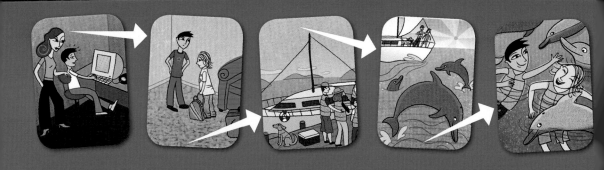

3 Think about . . .

including personal comments,

I wished things could be a little different

I'm sure he broke the sound barrier.

No way could this weed of a kid be the same age as me!

He reminded me of Havoc . . . greedily guzzling his breakfast.

using the first person,

my	I	me	our	we	us

using the past tense.

I was surfing the Net . . .   **Then I spotted it . . .**

Time galloped past.

4 Think about the conclusion.

Writing a Personal Recount

Have you . . .

- included your own responses and reactions?

- recorded the events in a sequence and made links to time?

- included events that all relate to one particular occasion, happening or idea?

- included a conclusion at the end that may have an interpretation of events or a personal comment?

- written your recount in the past tense?

- used the first person?

- personally involved yourself in the event?

> **Don't forget to revisit your writing. Do you need to change, add or delete anything to improve your story?**